To Rob Ream
with best regards!

Jeff Wayne

AMERICAN
WILDFOWL DECOYS

AMERICAN WILDFOWL DECOYS

JEFF WAINGROW
Photographs by Carleton Palmer
Foreword by Adele Earnest

E. P. DUTTON   NEW YORK
In association with the
MUSEUM OF AMERICAN FOLK ART   NEW YORK

Book design by Marilyn Rey

First published, 1985, in the United States by E. P. Dutton. / All rights reserved under International and Pan-American Copyright Conventions. / No part of this book may be reproduced or transmitted in any form or by any means, electronic or mechanical, including photocopy, recording, or any storage and retrieval system now known or to be invented, without permission in writing from the publishers, except by a reviewer who wishes to quote brief passages in connection with a review written for inclusion in a magazine, newspaper, or broadcast. / Published simultaneously in Canada by Fitzhenry & Whiteside Limited, Toronto. / W / Published in the United States by E. P. Dutton, a division of New American Library, 2 Park Avenue, New York, N.Y. 10016. / Printed and bound by Dai Nippon Printing Co., Ltd., Tokyo, Japan. / Library of Congress Catalog Card Number: 85-70844. / ISBN: 0-525-24367-4 (cloth); ISBN: 0-525-48185-0 (DP).
10 9 8 7 6 5 4 3 2 1 First Edition

CONTENTS

FOREWORD

My first wildfowl decoy I found on a beach, a Cape Cod beach, where I walked one spring day in 1953. There it was: a wooden bird standing at the edge of a salt marsh. As I picked it up, the stake broke in my hand.

Winsor White, an authority on decoys whom I had met, lived in Duxbury, not far from the Cape. With bird and courage in hand, I drove to his home, where he received me graciously. Yes, my carving was indeed a decoy, a yellowlegs shorebird, left and forgotten by some hunter years ago. The tacks on the bird's weathered surface showed where real feathers had once been attached.

The previous year Winsor White had attended the annual antiques show in White Plains, New York, where as a dealer in fine early furniture and accessories he had shocked the public by featuring decoys as "art," with price tags to suit. Winsor was always sure of his ground. Descended from original settlers in the Massachusetts Bay Colony, he disliked having his opinions or his prices questioned. He never dickered.

Years and miles after that first meeting, other fortuitous events stimulated my awareness of the wildfowl decoy as an art to be saved and honored. One winter I took a leisurely drive down the Atlantic coast from New England to the Carolinas. Along the way I stopped to inquire about decoys. In Maryland I rescued a swan decoy from a pile of burning rubbish. My first Lem Ward decoy I saw on a restaurant shelf keeping company with catsup bottles. If the decoy was really an art, it deserved to keep better company. Even its recent presence at New York antiques shows and at sportsmen's exhibitions was not enough recognition.

In 1959 my gallery in Stony Point, New York, presented an exhibition of decoys at the prestigious Willard Gallery in New York City. This was a first, a trial run for the decoy being shown as art at a metropolitan gallery. The museum response was immediate. The Abby Aldrich Rockefeller Folk Art Collection in Williamsburg, Virginia, purchased birds, and so did the Museum of Fine Arts in Boston, the Memorial Art Gallery in Rochester, New York, and the Munson-Williams-Proctor Institute in Utica, New York.

Because museums and collectors requested more specific information about decoys, I wrote a book in 1965 titled *The Art of the Decoy*, in which sources, regional characteristics, and distinctive traits of specific carvers were described. The book's cover featured a photograph of my first decoy, the yellowlegs I had found on the beach at Cape Cod.

In November 1965 the Museum of American Folk Art presented an exhibition of wildfowl decoys at its gallery on West Fifty-third Street in New York City. The show, which included loans from several collectors, featured birds from Winsor White's collection. When the exhibition closed, Alastair B. Martin purchased the nucleus of the White collection and presented the major portion— 140 decoys—as a gift to the museum. Thus the museum collection of wildfowl decoys was born.

In 1967 my selection of decoys from the museum's collection, plus some additional pieces, were packed, crated, and shipped to the Montreal World's Fair. There, in the United States Pavilion, our unique American folk art was introduced and revealed to an international audience.

In November 1969 The Metropolitan Museum of Art in New York City paid the decoy the ultimate honor. It placed on view in its

Blumenthal Patio Gallery four decoys from the private Guennol Collection owned by Alastair B. Martin: a pair of Red-breasted Mergansers by Lothrop T. Holmes of Kingston, Massachusetts; a Common Loon by Harvey Wass of Addison, Maine; and an eighteenth-century Mallard.

The Museum of American Folk Art takes great pride in its collection and in its early recognition of the wildfowl decoy as significant folk art. May we hope that many donors will continue to come bearing gifts to our museum, where American folk arts are shared, researched, and cared for in the safe harbor of our keeping.

ADELE EARNEST

INTRODUCTION

A number of years ago, I visited Vermont's Shelburne Museum—more specifically Dorset House, the charming old structure that contains the decoy collection. The museum grounds were empty and quiet as it was well past the tourist season, so any sounds nearby inevitably caught my attention. Soon I became aware that someone had apparently been sent ahead to report on the building's contents. After a quick turn through the front room, the scout returned to her friends with her report. There was really no point in coming in, she advised, for the entire building contained "nothing but a bunch of wooden ducks." Her words rattled around in my mind as I tried to return to my decoy investigations. Then I suddenly realized the full import of those words. To anyone who had not had the opportunity to learn otherwise, they really *were* just a bunch of unremarkable wooden birds.

Decoy making is a subtle art, a fact that is rarely appreciated by those with only a passing interest in the subject. Without a fuller understanding of how decoys have been made and used, one can't help responding much as the woman did at Dorset House. She, then, is perhaps as much the cause of my writing this book as anyone.

The collection of decoys at the Museum of American Folk Art contains a broad range of exceptional carvings. Space limitations required that many worthy examples be excluded from this book, yet those we have illustrated represent the collection admirably and provide a balance essential to the book's purposes. Also, although not every decoy shown should necessarily be assumed to be the best work from a particular carver or region, a large majority are in fact just that. The reader will also observe that many Massachusetts birds found their way into the book, which is a simple reflection of the strength of the museum's holdings from that area. I have tried neither to ignore this fact nor permit it to limit a fuller exploration of the field. On the other hand, no attempt has been made to be encyclopedic except as that word may imply a broadened perspective.

The order of the essays and accompanying illustrations is generally geographic, specifically a trip up the Atlantic coast from south to north. Although this arrangement is somewhat arbitrary, it does help to emphasize the importance of geographical influences on the ways decoys were made and used. Additionally, it enables us to proceed logically toward the climax of our decoy tour—New England.

Many books have already been written about decoys, and each has, to a greater or lesser extent, broadened our understanding of the subject. Generally, the approach has been to focus on matters of fact rather than of opinion. This has served quite well overall, for personal viewpoints should be presented only after facts become clear. I hope that time has now arrived, for in this book I have departed somewhat from tradition and drawn a more impressionistic picture of the field by combining fact and interpretation. With luck, this effort may help nurture a wider interest in an extraordinary American legacy and encourage more people to realize that decoys are, indeed, not just wooden ducks.

Any book about decoys must necessarily be influenced by many other writers and collectors. In this case, however, some people have made an even larger contribution. My particular thanks go first to Charles "Bud" Ward of Oceanside, New York, for his critical evaluation of the text. Additional help was generously given by Henry Fleckenstein of Cambridge, Maryland; Ted Harmon of West Barnstable, Massachusetts; John Hillman of Sea Girt, New Jersey; Dixon Merkt of Guilford, Connecticut; William Purnell of Ocean City, Maryland; and Bob White of Tullytown, Pennsylvania. I am especially indebted to Adele Earnest of Stony Point, New York, for giving inspiration and practical advice. Thanks are also due to Robert Bishop of the Museum of American Folk Art for his faith in the project and the support he offered along the way. Finally, gratitude is extended to my two working partners, Cyril I. Nelson of E. P. Dutton, whose professional and personal concern have been invaluable, and Carleton Palmer, whose photographic artistry and personal amiability added immeasurably to the pleasure of this endeavor.

JEFF WAINGROW

AMERICAN WILDFOWL DECOYS

BUFFLEHEAD HEN
Maker unidentified
c. 1960; Length, 9"

The charming Bufflehead illustrated on the opposite page inspires several thoughts on the subject of decoy collecting. Paramount among them is the simple fact that decoys were made as tools of the hunt and were never intended to serve as decorative objects.

Most modern carvings, on the other hand, are not meant for use in hunting, although superficially they may have the characteristics of working examples. Decoy collectors are inclined to call these pieces "decorative," a label not always intended as a compliment. In fact, however, the best decorative carvings can and should be admired both as art and craft, but they are wisely grouped separately from authentic working decoys.

The Bufflehead hen clearly belongs in the decorative category. While it is unquestionably from the hand of a skilled artist and even has many of the traits of a typical working bird, it is far too finely detailed to be practical. Add to this its unused condition and clearly recent vintage, and the evidence points to a category outside our real area of interest.

Authentic decoys for waterfowl gunning are, of course, still being made, mostly in small factories where handwork has largely been replaced by the efficiency of the duplicating lathe and the assembly line. These modern factory products are generally of limited concern to the collector, who favors instead the handmade examples that were used during the great era of wildfowl gunning.

The collectible decoy, then, must essentially be an individually made product intended for use in hunting. These pieces began appearing regularly in the early part of the nineteenth century, but their creation practically ceased by the 1950s as the old-time makers passed from the scene. In a sense, the collector's mission now is to help preserve these objects from an age that is gone forever.

WILLET
Mason Decoy Factory
Detroit, Michigan
c. 1900; Length, 14½″

Mechanization came to decoy making at first in a rudimentary way, with the earliest professional carvers adopting techniques that lent themselves to relatively simple repetition. A man might carve a large number of bodies, then heads, and finally paint a series of decoys section by section. The obvious advantage of this practice was the time saved in the preparation for each of these tasks and the economy that resulted from concentrating on only one job. The compelling logic of the assembly line, the creation of American industrial genius, began to find its application in the production of hunting decoys.

The earliest professional makers did indeed devise methods that simplified the task of producing what was by any standard a handmade decoy. Eventually, however, the duplicating lathe entered the picture, permitting small factories to shape decoy bodies with such rapidity that extensive advertising and sales were the result.

The term *factory* and its connotations somehow seem strangely inappropriate when referring to the earliest attempts to mass produce decoys. While the machinery for duplicating was clearly mechanical and required little human assistance, the rest of the decoy's construction and painting was still done with hand labor. The important distinction between the more familiar professional makers and the new factories that sprang up to help supply the sport hunters' needs was the greater standardization required by factory work. There, specialization of tasks reduced reliance on any particular worker and generally led to a more consistent product. The Mason Decoy Factory of Detroit, Michigan, was the most important of these early enterprises, and a study of its best work helps explain the substantial success it enjoyed.

8

LONG-BILLED CURLEW
Mason Decoy Factory
Detroit, Michigan
c. 1900; Length, 17″

For the collector, Mason decoys are a complete field of study in their own right. No other factory, nor for that matter any other professional decoy maker, has ever equaled Mason's range of species, and few have attained its standard of quality.

William J. Mason founded the Detroit company in 1896 and ran it continuously until 1924. During that time, a countrywide system of distribution made Mason decoys available in almost every state, creating a near-total dominance in the factory-decoy field. Success, however, was as much the result of an exceptional product as it was of business acumen. From the selection of wood and its turning on lathes to the choice of paints and their application, Masons stand apart from almost all other mass-produced decoys in the field. Even durability is a Mason trait, with few decoys developing cracks or splits and with painted surfaces even standing up to the punishing salt water of the Atlantic Ocean.

Mason decoys, both shorebirds and waterfowl, were manufactured in different grades, with the finest ones, the Premier and Challenge ducks and the glass-eyed shorebirds all displaying handsome fully developed bodies and expert paintwork. The curlew shown here represents the best from the Mason Factory; its graceful form and subtle painting being attractive to bird and man alike. Close examination of the paint reveals a special Mason signature common to all its decoys: paint was always applied with a deep texturing and in a swirl pattern that, once identified by the observant collector, will never be mistaken for any other maker's work. And confusion is sometimes more of a problem than one might imagine, since the Pratt Manufacturing Company of Joliet, Illinois, purchased the Mason Factory equipment in 1926. From that point on, Pratt decoys understandably bore a closer resemblance to Masons than ever before.

RUDDY DUCK
Ivey Stevens
Knotts Island, North Carolina
c. 1920; Length, 10½"

North Carolinians called them "boobies." Farther north on the Susquehanna Flats, "greasers" was the favored term. Commercial gunners, a none-too-sentimental lot, referred to them as "dollar ducks," an obvious reference to the market price. But whichever name it went by, the Ruddy Duck and North Carolina duck hunting were to become synonymous. In fact, more Ruddy decoys were made and used in the area of Currituck Sound, that state's famed wildfowl shooting ground, than anywhere else in the country.

The list of essentials for the proper Ruddy decoy includes a chunky body, a long full tail, and the inimitable Ruddy head and bill that immediately distinguish it from all other ducks. When these features are combined in pleasing proportions by a skilled craftsman, you have both an effective lure and a beguiling piece of sculpture. The best examples, such as those by Lem and Lee Dudley and by John Williams, may at times lean slightly toward the primitive, but they are never crude. That is an important distinction and one well understood by the maker of our saucy Ruddy, Ivey Stevens. He polished his skills when he joined with John Williams to produce what is now a highly regarded rig of Ruddy decoys for use near Knotts and Cedar islands.

Well-made Ruddy decoys have always enjoyed a considerable popularity. Two of the earliest and finest writers in the field, Joel Barber and William Mackey, Jr., freely expressed their admiration for what was even then a rare commodity. More recently, a group of knowledgeable collectors gathered at Shelburne Museum in Vermont to examine their impressive fifteen-hundred piece collection. Opinion was nearly unanimous when the time came to pick a favorite: it was a Ruddy from North Carolina.

Finding a good specimen today to add to your collection may present a substantial challenge. Ruddy decoys often saw hard use and many have not survived intact. Those that did, when blessed with that special Ruddy charm, fetch a premium. It is a price the knowledgeable collector will gladly pay.

SWAN
James R. Best
Kitty Hawk, North Carolina
c. 1910; Length, 22"

Most collectors want to own an old swan decoy, but there just aren't enough good ones to go around.

Back in the mid-nineteenth century, swan decoys were occasionally used to hunt the Trumpeter Swan, a bird prized for its down. (The Whistling Swan was shot mostly for sport, as only the young cygnet was fit to eat.) Later in the century, market hunters set out a few swans as "confidence decoys," that is, replicas of species other than the one being hunted. The intent of such decoys was to create a peaceful scene, so that flying ducks or geese would feel secure in settling among the decoys.

By 1913, the federal government had completely outlawed the shooting of swans, and market gunning was generally in decline. It was then that many swan decoys were converted to goose decoys by the replacement of heads and necks and by suitable repainting.

Today, swan decoys can still be seen bobbing among rigs of duck decoys along Chesapeake Bay, the Back Bay of Virginia, and in North Carolina on Currituck Sound, but their role is somewhat altered. Now, their presence is designed to signal to the ducks, widgeons especially, that food is available, for the swan's long neck allows it to rip plants from the bottom that ducks are unable to reach. The presence of swans usually means good eating for ducks.

For collectors, the most desirable swan decoys are from the market-hunting era, but few of those have survived intact. Add the fact that the necks were extremely vulnerable to breakage and you have the makings of a great scarcity. The swan decoy by James R. Best ranks with the finest of this rare type.

14

BLACK DUCK
Nathan Cobb
Cobb Island, Virginia
c. 1870; Length, 16"

The Cobb family was in for quite a surprise. As they were sailing south from Massachusetts in 1837, a severe storm deposited the whole group and their boat somewhat abruptly on the Eastern Shore of Virginia. Exactly how much farther they had intended to travel is not known, but they must have liked where they landed, for soon they had established a home. Eventually, they went on to purchase a seaside island called Sandy Shoals, which became known thereafter as Cobb Island. There were three Cobb sons, and Nathan is the one of principal interest to us as a decoy maker.

Through the industry of the Cobb family, the island eventually developed into a major resort, actually becoming the most famous one south of Atlantic City during the mid-nineteenth century. Its favored ocean setting, as well as its unequaled fishing and wildfowl gunning, attracted so many enthusiasts that at its height Cobb Island even boasted a church and a bowling alley.

Nathan Cobb worked hard to supply the steady stream of visiting gunners with decoys, the quality of which was unmatched in the region. Both his and the resort's fame spread widely, and the demand eventually surpassed Nathan's ability to satisfy it. This forced him and his son Elkenah to purchase decoys from, among others, the famed Tuckerton, New Jersey, maker Harry V. Shourds. As a result, the Cobb name is often found branded on these and other New Jersey decoys.

In 1890, a hurricane roared up the Atlantic coast, striking the island squarely and leveling it. Not a building remained standing, and the survivors moved what little there was left back to the mainland. The Nathan Cobb decoys went back also, drifting over on their own, to be picked up by people who knew a good thing when it floated by. Perhaps the Black Duck pictured here was once part of that famous fleet.

HUDSONIAN CURLEW
Nathan Cobb
Cobb Island, Virginia
c. 1870; Length, 16"

Of all the demanding tasks facing the decoy maker, none is more difficult than giving the carved wooden decoy a sense of life and movement. In fact, few carvers have ever been inclined really to address this problem and fewer still have been its master, for neither a concern with superficial beauty nor with surface realism proves a satisfactory answer.

Nathan Cobb, the object of our attention here, was one of the best at creating, through the deft manipulation of posture and gesture, a sense of the live bird. This he accomplished principally by the skillful carving and joining of heads and bodies. The way the two elements interacted was highly expressive, much more than would be apparent when each part was examined separately. More remarkable still is that none of this was achieved by resorting to precise or fussy detailing.

More thought, effort, and care went into each Nathan Cobb decoy than might be immediately obvious to the neophyte. From his expert choice of woods to his willingness to spare no expense for such desirable materials as German taxidermist's eyes and brass screws, Nathan Cobb unquestionably influenced others on and off Cobb Island with his extraordinary standards of quality. Even more important, however, was Cobb's brilliant use of old, weathered holly-tree roots as heads and necks on his Canada Goose and Brant decoys. This nearly grainless wood possessed a strength no other material could match, and with a little artful shaping, Cobb was able to make heads and necks with long sinuous shapes that could still withstand the rigors of heavy use. When these were mated with Cobb's well-formed bodies, they displayed such expressive attitudes that, as a group, they stand alone in the world of decoys. This same quality of animation is also immediately apparent in the Cobb ducks and shorebirds with conventionally carved heads, proof that Nathan Cobb's special genius touched all his work.

LEAST SANDPIPER
Dave "Umbrella" Watson
Chincoteague Island, Virginia
c. 1910; Length, 6½"

The last century saw its share of individualists, and Dave "Umbrella" Watson surely led the Chincoteague Island parade. When queried as to why he carried an umbrella in both good weather and bad, he allowed that only a fool would be without one when it started to rain. This logic must have applied equally to his rubber boots, for he was never seen without those either. The reaction of the locals to these peculiarities is lost now, but surely they must have admired the man whose carvings rank as that island's most finely crafted.

Until recently, many collectors believed that a sandpiper decoy like the one pictured here was made at the lighthouse station in Loveladies, New Jersey. The great authority William Mackey, Jr., made this attribution, and not until recently have perceptive Virginia collectors come to identify the sandpipers as the work of Umbrella Watson. Interestingly, this error may illustrate not so much the shortcomings of an exceptional decoy scholar as the tendency of most of us to accept what we hear repeated often enough.

Watson was born in 1851 and spent his life around Chincoteague as a waterman, hunter, and guide for sport gunners. Relatively few of his decoys are found today, which leads one to guess that such finely crafted work was bought at a premium and was not available to the average hunter. Evidence for this assumption comes partially from the *Gooseville Gun Club* brand found on many of his ducks. Apparently, his audience was the sport hunter, for only he would be likely to support Dave's preference for using expensive white pine when the countryside overflowed with fine cedar.

Watson's shorebirds pay homage to the Virginia carving traditions: a ridge down the back right to the tail, raised-wing carving forming a distinct V, and oak bills with flat undersides neatly inserted through the head and splined at the rear. What separates his decoys from the work of others is their distinctive heads and, especially in the case of his "peeps" (sandpipers), an overfed look that so charmingly mimics those delightful creatures that scurry along the beach. Watson's ducks are anomalies for the region because of their wood, their hollow bodies, and their especially fine workmanship. As with all his other decoys, they are a mirror of their maker, a singular spirit.

20

CANADA GOOSE
Ira Hudson
Chincoteague Island, Virginia
c. 1920; Length, 25″

The peninsula narrows south from Delaware and Maryland as you cross over into Virginia. Close by the shore on the Atlantic side sits Chincoteague Island, once the home of Virginia's most prolific decoy maker, Ira Hudson.

Until recently, Chincoteague and adjacent Assateague islands maintained little contact with the mainland. The hardy souls who lived there earned a livelihood primarily from the water, although wildfowl sport and market gunning quite early became an integral part of the island economy. Chincoteague boasts a disproportionately large number of talented carvers for such a modest population and none was better known than Ira Hudson. His reputation rests largely on his duck, goose, and shorebird decoys, said to number as many as twenty-five thousand during a long career. Not to be ignored, however, are his decorative bird and fish carvings and a much-admired and widely used boat he called a "dead rise batteau."

A small book would be required to describe adequately the tremendous range of styles Hudson created. Collectors have identified nine or ten distinct forms of Black Duck decoys alone. He willingly used any available wood—cedar, balsa, cypress, pine—and expended as much effort as the customer was willing to subsidize. Ira's son Delbert remembers his father mentioning that he sold some duck decoys for as little as three dollars a dozen at the beginning of the century.

All of Ira Hudson's decoys were capably carved and painted, yet when the mood struck or a flush sportsman commissioned something special, he truly excelled. Perhaps that's how this Canada Goose came into existence, for it has all the hallmarks of the best Virginia work. Hudson's ability to rise above the mundane requirements of a difficult life as often as he did ensures his reputation as Virginia's most important carver.

LESSER YELLOWLEGS
Charles Clark
Chincoteague Island, Virginia
c. 1920; Length, 10"

Hardly a collector alive has failed to express an opinion about Charles Clark's shorebirds. Most feel strongly one way or the other. Whichever way you're inclined, it's difficult not to admit that these decoys have personality. To some, however, the outsize bodies (or is it the undersize heads?) are merely laughable, not much more than caricatures of the live birds. Others, however, respond more positively to the awkward folk charm of Clark's carvings. It is probably best to allow personal taste to be the final arbiter of this question.

Clark's shorebirds have had a curious history. For a number of years they were thought to be the work of William Matthews, a Chincoteague, Virginia, hunter known to have gunned over a rather extensive and varied rig of locally made shorebirds. Early research concluded that all decoys in the Matthews rig were carved by him, an error corrected when Clark was established as the maker.

Because a sizable number of Charles Clark's decoys are found in nearly perfect original condition, many collectors now believe that they were made both before and after the shooting of shorebirds was outlawed in 1918. William Mackey, Jr., the dean of decoy collectors, noted that on walks down Main Street in Chincoteague during the 1930s, one could see dozens of Clark's shorebirds propped up in flower gardens and on lawns. He confessed that "at a dollar or two apiece, I moved as many of them out of the gardens as good taste dictated to decorate another environment." There's a pretty good chance that if you have one of Charles Clark's shorebirds in your collection, it is because of these Main Street transactions, and very possibly a pink flamingo now stands in its place!

LONG-BILLED CURLEW
Robert Andrews
Smith Island, Virginia
c. 1910; Length, 17"

Those with only a casual interest in decoys often ask, when referring to a particular carving, whether or not it was signed by the maker. Experienced collectors know from having examined the undersides of thousands of decoys that very few ever carried a carver's mark. There was a good reason for this.

Hunters found over the course of a season that it wasn't at all uncommon to lose a decoy or two to a fast-moving river or a rough sea. To be able to reclaim them at a later date, owners often branded the bottoms of the decoys and this generally served as proof of ownership. Decoy makers appreciated this fact and most often did not confuse the issue with their own brands. Yet there were notable exceptions: Lothrop Holmes (Kingston, Massachusetts) and Ferdinand Bach (Detroit River, Michigan) carefully marked their pieces with their full names, while Nathan Cobb (Cobb Island, Virginia), Lou Barkelow (Forked River, New Jersey), and Luther Nottingham (Cape Charles, Virginia) limited themselves to initials. Some commercial makers succumbed to the temptation to have each decoy serve as an advertisement. In the Midwest, Bert Graves (Peoria, Illinois), Charles Perdew (Henry, Illinois), and Robert Elliston (Bureau, Illinois) each stamped his name on long lead weights. Back east, Elmer Crowell (East Harwich, Massachusetts) went further and, except for his earliest work, employed a series of oval and rectangular brands that now help us to date his work fairly exactly.

Despite these examples, however, the remarkable fact remains that most carvers, even those who whittled only a few for their own use; did not put their names on their decoys. Exactly how they curbed the temptation to claim their due recognition remains unanswered, but one supposes it is because of the inherent modesty of the carvers.

It is no criticism of Robert Andrews to observe that he simply could not resist inscribing his swoopy curlew decoy with an appropriately bold *R* on the underside of the tail. Today, it actually pleases us to see evidence of such justifiable pride.

26

PINTAIL DRAKE
Steve and Lem Ward
Crisfield, Maryland
c. 1935; Length, 18"

By the start of the Depression, business had slowed considerably at the Ward brothers' barbershop in Crisfield, Maryland. Hard times had come to town, and the local citizens found themselves cutting back to bare essentials. While this proved no help to the barbering business, it did wonders for anyone who could make an effective decoy and sell it at a fair price, for hunting had become one of the best ways to put food on the table. In earlier years, the Wards had made fewer than a hundred decoys annually, mostly for their own use. Now they had all they could do to keep up with the demand.

Crisfield, situated on the western side of the peninsula near the Virginia line, has a tradition of decoy making extending well back into the last century. Through the years, a distinctive style evolved that is completely different from the typical Chesapeake Bay decoy found nearby. It's as if the town were insulated from the surrounding traditions by some power of creative will. The Ward brothers had always been comfortable with this Crisfield style

but not with the quality of the local product. With Steve as the carver and Lem as the painter, they altered the course of Crisfield decoy making by producing more ingeniously conceived and masterfully executed decoys than all the other carvers combined. Even their most plebeian effort displayed such a jaunty style and realistic character that their reputation quickly spread in all directions. It seemed as if the Wards would never be satisfied, always striving to create a new look, a new style that would ever more closely mirror the live bird.

Later in their careers, in the 1950s, the Wards stopped carving decoys for the most part and turned their attention to ornamental work. With duck hunting in decline and Canvasback shooting outlawed, the brothers discovered a new world of endeavor. Today, collectors find virtually any carving by the Ward brothers desirable, but none more so than the glorious working decoy of a Pintail drake pictured. It shows them at their very best.

BROADBILL DRAKE
John Blair
Philadelphia, Pennsylvania
c. 1890; Length, 14″

A hundred years ago in the city of Philadelphia, a decoy mystery was in the making. It certainly wasn't planned, nor did the participants have any reason to suspect that a century later, a then-unknown breed—the decoy collector—would seek its solution. It would have been simple had John Blair carved his decoys in one recognizable style and also painted them, but then there wouldn't be the current confusion. The problem is caused by there being three quite distinctive styles of decoys, all displaying the exquisite brushstrokes of another man, Blair's friend, who was apparently a trolley-car decorator. So accomplished was this duck decoy painter that his work knows no equal even to this day. The same can fairly be said of John Blair's carving, and thus the interest in a partnership that is unlike any other in decoy annals.

Now back to the mystery. Simply stated, it turns on two central questions. First, why would Blair make decoys in three clearly distinguishable styles? Perhaps other carvers were also responsible? Second, how would a man who painted trolley cars have the time to paint many hundreds of decoys, for surely more were painted than have survived? Much has been written about this puzzle, most of it taking the form of elaborate speculations that have little basis in fact. Interestingly, Blair's grandson, John Blair III of Elkton, Maryland, remembers his grandfather and has some of his decoys, all of the best style now known as "classic" Blairs. He has never seen any of the other types, which may mean that the artist painted more than one carver's decoys. Perhaps it is wise to end the discussion here, for without some additional documentation, further speculation cannot be productive.

If you possess a Blair decoy with the qualities of the hollow broadbill shown here, rejoice, for you have a "classic" Blair. None finer ever rode the waters of the lower Delaware and none better is likely to grace your collection.

PINTAIL DRAKE
Maker unidentified
Delaware River area
c. 1930; Length, 18″

Although the Delaware River divides New Jersey and Pennsylvania, it has united decoy carvers from both sides for over a century. From Trenton south to Delaware Bay, one finds a decoy specially designed to suit a unique style of hunting.

Gunning from blinds was common in most regions, but not on the Delaware. Sculling was the method employed here, and it merits a brief description. It began with the hunter setting his rig of decoys well out into the river between the main channel and shore. He then rowed upstream to a point where he could observe ducks landing among the decoys. When they did, he slowly and cautiously sculled the boat to within range. If his decoys were sufficiently realistic, the live ducks would be held long enough for him to complete the approach. An effective paint pattern and close conformation to species became essential attributes of an effective lure.

During the 1930s, dredging of the river produced a swifter-flowing current, and the generally small and round-bottomed Delaware decoys foundered badly in the rushing waters. A new form quickly emerged, exemplified by the Pintail shown here. This new breed sported a substantially larger body with a flat bottom that permitted it to remain steady against the current. Carvers had adjusted to changing demands while retaining the attributes of the classic Delaware River decoy that still remained useful. This adaptation well personified the spirit of life near the water, where one's survival depended upon a willingness to keep what worked and change what didn't.

RUDDY TURNSTONE
Maker unidentified
New Jersey
c. 1900; Length, 8½"

Collectors in search of the rare and beautiful would do well to consider decoys for the Ruddy Turnstone. Brightly colored and distinctive, these charming short-necked birds are found from Canada to Florida. As they are nearly inedible, the birds were of little interest to the market hunter, and so they were shot primarily for sport. Why the majority of these "Calico-back" decoys came only from the southern part of New Jersey is still a mystery; in other regions, they are exceedingly rare.

Turnstone is an apt name, for the birds frequent the pebbly beaches of bays rather than the clear sandy stretches that border the ocean. Here they industriously poke and pry at stones until they locate a tidbit. While this constitutes the normal Turnstone diet, the annual spawning of the horseshoe crab provides the Ruddy with a special treat as the eggs wash ashore and lodge among rocks and pebbles.

New Jersey, the state that is the logical hunting ground for Turnstone decoys, had no truly commanding shorebird carver, although the work of Shourds, Leeds, and Barkelow merits high praise. In fact, this state's shorebird decoys, taken as a group, are generally anonymous and nonconformist. In contrast to the local duck decoys, stick-ups display such an enormous range of styles that even making a proper regional identification is sometimes difficult. The knowledgeable collector accepts this and still admires the exquisite workmanship and expressiveness of the best carvings.

If a decision is made to narrow one's collecting sights substantially, the choice of a specific species of shorebird may be appropriate. That idea leads us back to the original object of our attention, the Ruddy Turnstone. Since these are uncommon decoys, it requires a disciplined collector to accept such restricted choices and chances. If you are not that person, but do favor shorebirds, then the more commonly found yellowlegs and plover decoys offer more promising possibilities. Selecting the best from among a number of species greatly improves one's chances to assemble a representative sampling of the decoy maker's art.

LEAST SANDPIPER
Joel Barkelow
Forked River, New Jersey
c. 1900; Length, 7"

The Least Sandpiper is unquestionably the tamest of shorebirds, happily sharing his domain with any and all who happen by. Gentle in disposition, he betrays little fear of man, gladly going about his business of unearthing minute particles of food and singing his loud, sweet *treep*.

These "peeps" normally congregate in large flocks wherever suitable habitats are found around the country. They prefer mud flats, lake shores, marshy meadows, creeks, and flooded fields, just as long as some grassy cover is nearby. Except for their annual breeding migration northward to Canada and Alaska in May that lasts several months, they generally remain at their accustomed haunts.

To observe these sparrow-size shorebirds is to marvel that they were hunted at all. In fact, their unwary nature and willingness to return over and over to a hunter's decoys made them the easiest of targets. However, most hunters preferred the more attractive wildfowl gunning, which provided tastier eating and a greater challenge than the hapless and unappetizing sandpiper. Professional hunters also set their sights on the more marketable species and gunned the smaller shorebirds mostly on cold mornings when they were inclined to bunch together in large numbers. The carnage that ensued makes a dreary story now, although one struggles to remember that the values and perceptions of this earlier time were certainly very different from our own.

No history is available today for Joel Barkelow, but his decoy-making skills are apparent to anyone who examines his work. Quality of this kind is uncommon, particularly in the smaller shorebird decoys, for even the crudest ones were generally effective in attracting the unwitting live birds.

CANADA GOOSE
Nathan Rowley Horner
West Creek, New Jersey
c. 1925; Length, 24"

Tuckerton, New Jersey, a town located just west of Little Egg Harbor, has been an important port for the south-central region of the state since the late eighteenth century. To the decoy collector, however, it is better known as the center of a school of carving that boasts such famous names as Harry V. Shourds, Ellis Parker, Rhoades Truax, Chris Sprague, and Horner. Here we find a decoy that differs little among makers. Typically featured is a two-piece cedar body of remarkable thinness known throughout the decoy world as the New Jersey "dugout."

Rowley Horner, the maker of the Canada Goose shown opposite, was born in Tuckerton in 1882 and later moved to nearby West Creek, where he built boats, clammed, served as a guide for groups of gunners, and of course, made decoys. It is even said that he was a competent musician, performing at movie theaters and dance halls in the area. Students of decoy lore naturally enjoy these bits and pieces of history, but it is really the Horner decoys that please collectors most.

In Tuckerton, Harry V. Shourds was without doubt the most important professional carver. Horner, in a sense his successor, took the classic Tuckerton style of decoy that Shourds already made so well and developed an even more natural look through a series of subtle refinements. It can be stated with little fear of dispute that Rowley Horner produced the finest group of duck, goose, and Brant decoys of any New Jersey maker. Examination of a representative group of Horner decoys confirms this judgment. Unfortunately, finding good examples of Horner's artistry isn't an easy task, for he was not especially prolific. There was one exception: a brilliant collaboration with Chris Sprague and Horner's uncle, Ellis Parker, in 1935, when the three carvers joined forces and assigned tasks to make a large and now famous rig that many senior collectors feel epitomizes the best from New Jersey. The Canada Goose pictured here is not from that rig, but it is certainly representative of Horner's finest work.

DOWITCHER
William Bowman
Possibly Bangor, Maine, area
c. 1890; Length, 10½″

Remarkably little is known about the greatest carver of shorebirds who ever lived. Researchers at the Museums at Stony Brook, Long Island, have unearthed some fascinating bits of census data indicating that a William H. Bowman (1824–1906) lived in Old Town, Maine (just north of Bangor), and worked as a millman. They also located an obituary notice corresponding to the time Bowman is said to have stopped visiting the Long Island marshes where he gunned. This connection was confirmed after a rig of twenty exemplary Bowman shorebirds and the Lawrence, Long Island, family that used them—the Herricks—were located. They had known Bill Bowman and were able to confirm that he was actually from the Bangor, Maine, area. Whether the two Bill Bowmans are in fact the same person is not certain, but this type of circumstantial evidence is fairly convincing. Except for a few other recollections in print about Bowman's carving and drinking exploits, which seem mostly the product of a lively imagina-

tion, nothing more is currently known. By the way, the Herricks later gave those wonderful shorebirds to the Museums at Stony Brook, where they are now permanently displayed.

Now to the matter of Bowman's decoys and what makes them so extraordinary. Unfortunately, words are not fully equal to this task, for Bowman's shorebirds really need to be held to be fully appreciated. Quite simply, no other carver so effectively captured in wood the contours of the live bird. With eyes closed and Bill's work in hand, confusion with other makers' decoys is nearly impossible. The details—realistic German taxidermists' eyes; a refined paint palette of dusty tans, grays, browns, and blacks; exquisitely carved wing tips and other refinements—somehow convey less of the specialness of these pieces than one wishes. It is probably better just to observe that only Elmer Crowell, the Cape Cod master, was a better shorebird painter, and that Bill Bowman's carving stands alone.

LESSER YELLOWLEGS
Attributed to Smith Clinton Verity
Seaford, Long Island, New York
c. 1900; Length, 10½"

Thirty miles of tidal ponds and salt marsh line the south shore of Long Island from Jamaica Bay on the west to the Great South Bay on the east, separated from the Atlantic Ocean by a narrow barrier beach. On the mainland side, fishing villages dot the coast. Together, this remarkable region constitutes a wildfowl and gunner's paradise.

During the last century, Seaford (at that time named Verity Town) was the center for the area, and it was in that town and its environs that some of the most exceptional shorebirds from any region were made. Although he was not the first, Obediah Verity was the leading practitioner of this local art. The graceful feeding-yellowlegs decoy pictured here is thought to be by Smith Clinton Verity, Obediah's brother; but this is only an educated guess.

Seaford shorebirds share a number of characteristics, the most notable being carved eyes, an S-shaped, raised-wing pattern typically joining in a V at the tail, and a distinctive style of painting that requires a brief description. Usually, a twig was broken off and chewed to form a crude paintbrush; when dipped into a dark paint color and daubed gently onto a lighter ground color in a series of successive partial circles, it created the useful illusion of feathering. Much of the local production was of yellowlegs and plover, though Sanderlings, curlews, terns, Knots, and Turnstones are all known. Most were carved in a conventional pose, so those few yellowlegs and plover in feeding postures are sought with special avidity. In fact, almost any shorebird from the area is highly collectible, for as most advanced collectors will agree, there was a consistently high standard set in that small town that knows no equal in the entire world of decoys.

COMMON GOLDENEYE DRAKE
Attributed to T. Smith
Possibly western New York State
c. 1920; Length, 13½″

The collecting spirit is nearly as old as man himself, and it has played a substantial role in the advancement of our knowledge of decoys and the life surrounding their use.

The wish to acquire an exceptional decoy is in the best sense a desire truly to possess it: meaning, to know it and its history and all that went into its creation as thoroughly as possible. This is a striving toward real connoisseurship. In the world of wildfowl carvings, it is natural for collectors to respond strongly to the allure of a classically beautiful decoy that rewards the senses with a maker's mastery of form and embellishment. The pleasure from collecting such decoys is readily apparent, but their acquisition normally requires a substantial investment of money. A promising alternative is to choose more unconventional carvings, such as the Goldeneye decoy illustrated here.

Unfortunately, details about the life of the man who carved this Goldeneye appear to be irretrievably lost, so that it is impossible even to document his name at this late date. The only thing certain is that the carver captured a Goldeneye in a way no one has before or since. Note the incongruity between this curious fellow's head and body: although the body is expertly crafted, it is nevertheless conventional in style and form. It functions as a kind of foil for the marvelously improbable head, and its simplicity prevents the decoy from appearing grotesque. Ultimately, the seemingly disparate elements happily combine to form a lively, charming, collectible decoy.

BLACK DUCK
Charles "Shang" Wheeler
Stratford, Connecticut
c. 1930; Length, 17½"

Not until Albert Laing arrived in Stratford, Connecticut, in 1863 did the hunters from this town near the mouth of the Housatonic River realize what they had been missing. For Laing started a decoy-making revolution the effects of which are still felt, more than one hundred years later.

Before the Civil War, Stratford decoys were of the so-called rocking-horse type, heavy and nondescript solid-body pieces that had little to recommend them. Laing's beginnings in New Jersey apparently influenced him in his new surroundings, for the Jersey dugout-style hollow body became part of Laing's new Stratford model. More significant still were two unusual refinements that over the years have proved themselves completely. First, Laing realized that the often slushy and icy currents on the Housatonic caused a decoy with a low breast to load up and tip down into the water. The solution was a high, puffed-out breast that rode serenely over the ice. Then Laing did something even more startling for the time, which was to vary the positions of the heads and necks so that a more realistic rig of naturally posed decoys could be assembled on the water. This became another enduring characteristic of decoys from the Stratford, Connecticut, area, and Charles "Shang" Wheeler was its most artful interpreter.

Wheeler followed in the tradition of Laing and the third great Stratford carver, Benjamin Holmes, by adhering to the high standards of craftsmanship and the proven methods that the other two had established, while raising the Stratford duck decoy to a still grander level of elegance and refinement. His legacy can be seen in the handsome, decorative Black Duck on the opposite page.

CANVASBACK DRAKE
Charles "Shang" Wheeler
Stratford, Connecticut
c. 1930; Length, 16″

Shang Wheeler was a Connecticut man for all seasons. While best known as a decoy maker, Wheeler also carved exquisite life-size fish, meticulously formed ship half-models, and lifelike decorative birds. He even tried his hand at drawing and painting, regularly contributing topical cartoons to local newspapers. Yet these were merely pastimes, ways to fill the spare moments during the long days he put in as manager of a major oyster-farming business in his hometown of Stratford.

In the 1920s, Wheeler launched a political career that took him to the Connecticut house of representatives and later to the state senate, although his motivation seemed born less of political ambition than of a desire to see stronger conservation laws enacted. His true love was the outdoors, especially when it included a fishing or hunting campsite and the easy camaraderie of his companions. Here, one guesses, Wheeler was most in his element, tying flies for fishing, exchanging tales, or setting out his incomparable decoys.

Wheeler never sold a decoy. All that he made were either used by him or given away to friends, and the time he spent on each was determined solely by its intended use. Some he entered in decoy-carving contests, and invariably he earned the top award. One of his Mallard drakes won the grand championship in the first American decoy show ever held, in Bellport, Long Island, in 1923. The suave pair of Canvasback decoys shown on the next two pages was never intended to be entered in competition. They are simply excellent working examples, although their appeal to collectors and to live birds would certainly not be lost on a contest judge.

CANVASBACK HEN
Charles "Shang" Wheeler
Stratford, Connecticut
c. 1930; Length, 15"

Experienced hunters have always admired decoys that are both strong and light. The importance of these qualities is obvious, and the nearly universal method by which they are simultaneously realized is through the use of the hollow wooden-decoy body. The style probably finds its origins in the famed New Jersey dugout decoy, where two pieces of wood, roughly equal in size, were hollowed, shaped, and finally nailed together to form the body. By 1900 the hollow form was to be found in many regions, the widespread acceptance ample proof of its worth. But there was a real drawback to this style: it required a considerable expenditure of time and effort to construct such a decoy. If badly done, rapid deterioration and eventual leakage were inevitable. Some makers discovered an ingenious alternative.

On Long Island in the late nineteenth century, carvers began using natural cork for decoy bodies, sometimes attaching boards on the bottom to add strength and thickness. The natural cork color, particularly when darkened, proved a convincing copy of the plumage of certain species, although paint was used also. Cork was an easily shaped and naturally buoyant material, perhaps more commonly used later in its pressed form than in its natural state, but nonetheless readily at hand. On occasion, cork could even be salvaged from old life preservers, a fact not lost on those who spent time close to the water.

Some of Shang Wheeler's cork-bodied decoys, like his pair of Canvasbacks, are the finest of their type ever made. With them, he compensated for the structural weakness of the cork by using only the best grade available to form the full, round bodies. When graced with one of Wheeler's masterfully carved and painted heads, the result was a decoy that satisfied every requirement for an effective lure.

BLACK DUCK
Charles "Shang" Wheeler
Stratford, Connecticut
c. 1930; Length, 18"

"There has always been a question between gunners as to whether or not there was any real difference in the attracting power of a rig of motley, ill-shaped blocks and a setting of decoys that really looked like ducks. Some claimed that birds would come to any kind of a flock, while others asserted that ducks could tell the difference and would decoy much better to a bunch of well-shaped, nicely painted decoys. Of course, there is nothing that resembles a live Mallard as much as another live Mallard. But inasmuch as live decoys are tabooed, the next best thing is something that resembles the live bird, and it has been the experience of the writer that in actual competition with several rigs of inferior decoys, the ducks chose to come to the bunch of superior decoys."

When Shang Wheeler wrote those words in 1947 in an essay titled "Long Island Sound," ducks and geese were already highly wary creatures whose ranks had been drastically reduced over the years by heavy hunting. Wheeler went on to speculate that the approaching ducks must perceive the difference between stiffly posed decoys, bobbing and pitching unnaturally in the water, and an array of realistically carved and painted ones created in natural postures, which rode smoothly. The latter, he felt, reassured the live ducks of the quiet and safety of the setting. Wheeler knew that with the thinning flocks and more restrictive laws governing bag limits and gunning seasons, the hunter's skill and guile alone would not be enough to compensate for inferior decoys. Better ones, in his eyes, had now become a necessity. This must surely have been to Wheeler the happy confirmation of an instinct that had guided his decoy making from the start.

WHITE-WINGED SCOTER DRAKE
Charles "Shang" Wheeler
Stratford, Connecticut
c. 1930; Length, 15"

October and November represent the height of the White-winged Scoter's migration southward, and for decades Stratford, Connecticut, hunters have set out their rigs of decoys in wait for these vividly marked black-and-white sea ducks. The scoters and their deep-sea brethren are commonly termed "divers." Some of them are known to plunge a hundred feet and more in search of the mollusks and other small animal life that typically constitute their diet. The word *diver* is somewhat misleading, for these ducks actually swim to the bottom using their feet, and the White-winged Scoter uses its wings.

Sea ducks tend to be larger than marsh ducks, also known as "dabblers," which usually feed on plant life in shallower fresh waters. Decoys generally tend to be made life-size, both because this makes a more accurate portrayal and also because larger decoys ride better in heavy seas. The commonest divers are the Canvasbacks, Common Goldeneyes, Greater Scaups, Lesser Scaups, Redheads, Common Eiders, and Oldsquaws. Mallards, Black Ducks, Pintails, American Widgeons, and Green- and Blue-winged Teal are the familiar dabblers. Mergansers occupy a third ornithological category and are found both inland and on the ocean. They are the fish eaters, and most hunters will testify that they generally make unpleasant eating. Ducks whose diets are composed largely of mollusks or crustaceans, like the White-winged Scoter's, are more edible than the mergansers, although most people prefer eating ducks that feed on grain and aquatic plants.

54

BRANT
Joseph W. Lincoln
Accord, Massachusetts
c. 1920; Length, 20"

The coast of Massachusetts that runs from Boston south nearly to Cape Cod has always been an area rich in wildfowl, and the decoy arts prospered there. In fact, many of the most inventive and beautifully made decoys from any region began their lives in towns that hug this shore. Foremost among the region's carvers was Joe Lincoln, a part-time professional maker who crafted some of the smoothest, simplest, and most elegant decoys anywhere. Lincoln began carving as a boy in his home town of Accord, Massachusetts, and soon discovered that he could make almost anything he liked with great success.

The decoys from Lincoln's mature period are notable for a fine restraint in both the carving and painting, with remarkable symmetry and fine finish work being his signature. Most species hunted in the region were part of his production, and every example he made conformed to his exceedingly high standards. Lincoln was in reality a purist, stubbornly shunning the machine tools that eventually became commonplace, relying instead on the familiar, old-time decoy-making implements: hatchet, drawknife, spoke shave, and rasp.

The Brant shown here possesses all the wonderful Lincoln traits, with his expert feel for scale and proportion obvious to the quickest glance. Never to be found is a fussy detail or an exaggerated feature, only the essentials for a perfectly realized decoy.

GREATER YELLOWLEGS
Joseph W. Lincoln
Accord, Massachusetts
c. 1910; Length, 12″

It is a paradox that so much is known about Joe Lincoln's duck and goose decoys and yet so little about his shorebirds. Actually, there is uncertainty about a number of carvings that may or may not be by Lincoln. That Lincoln made shorebirds is no longer questioned, for they were documented in an 1898 diary kept by his friend, Herbert Hatch. Reference was made there to the Greater and Lesser Yellowlegs decoys Lincoln had carved for him. We now know that plover and Ruddy Turnstone decoys should be added to this list of species.

When Lincoln began carving in the 1870s, all his decoys, including the shorebirds, possessed thin bodies and a rather primitive feeling. Eventually, fuller-bodied and smoother-finished decoys evolved, the kind that helped build Lincoln's fame. While there are a few examples of his later hollow work in collections, the solid-body yellowlegs shown here is more typical, and exemplary of his finest style. It is unmistakably a Lincoln. At the same time, there exists another group of shorebirds having many similarities to Lincoln's work, but they are more roughly carved and covered with knife marks. Collectors have argued interminably about the attribution of these particular pieces, with no firm conclusion. Commonly heard, however, is this telling point: if these pieces were not made by Lincoln, who else in the region was that talented and prolific? This argument is a strong one, but it alone can never ultimately serve as proof of authorship.

OLDSQUAW DRAKE
Joseph W. Lincoln
Accord, Massachusetts
c. 1920; Length, 14"

The bottom of a decoy is often a good place to begin learning more about it, and Joe Lincoln's Oldsquaw drake helps prove the point. Immediately apparent is a long, wide split on the underside running the length of the body. This "checking" of the wood is a common flaw in solid-body decoys, particularly when the wood is not well seasoned. While Lincoln was more careful than many in this regard, his use of solid-cedar heartwood made some checking almost unavoidable. Today's collector will learn to accept a certain amount of splitting in old decoys, especially when they are otherwise desirable and the cracks are not disfiguring. In the case of less important examples or of substantial damage, good sense advises one to pass these pieces by, as no amount of restoration will prove a successful cure for this problem.

A brand on the bottom of the decoy can also be a revealing feature. In this case, the brand *C. F. Spear Scituate* identifies Lincoln's friend and gunning part-ner Chester Spear of Scituate Harbor, Massachusetts, whose name is also found on many other Lincoln decoys. Brands for individual hunters and those for gun clubs are useful in helping connect decoys with their users, thus giving a clearer picture of the general distribution of a particular maker's work.

Clues to the original paint colors of repainted decoys can also often be discovered by scrutinizing the undersides. Even when there is substantial over-painting, the surface under the typical lead weight will normally reveal the original paint. Methods of construction become apparent too when the bottom of the decoy is observed: in this example, it is Lincoln's way of securing the head to the body.

The lesson then is a simple but important one: the bottom of a decoy should be studied just as carefully as the top.

BLACK DUCK
Joseph W. Lincoln
Accord, Massachusetts
c. 1920; Length, 18″

New Englanders seem to take special pride in their reputation for being both industrious and individualistic. Joe Lincoln was certainly of this breed. Few are aware, for instance, that Lincoln never limited himself just to decoy making, but was also actively involved with other trades and pastimes throughout a long and productive life. Even his efforts as a backyard gardener were a great success, for the dahlias he grew were consistent prize winners at various garden shows in Boston. Lincoln was a man of great energy and talent, and nowhere was this more apparent than in his decoys. A brief review of the range of forms he produced gives a sense of the uncommon breadth of his enterprise.

The Lincoln decoys are conveniently divided into two grades, the simpler of which he called "field grade" and the more elaborate ones, sometimes with hollow bodies or carved wings, "sporting grade." This system was eventually used for both shorebird and duck decoys, with nearly every locally hunted species represented. Canada Geese were by far the biggest sellers, and most of these had solid bodies, although a few were the oversize frame type with either a canvas, or later, a slat covering. The purpose of these so-called loomers was to draw the live geese nearer to the rig so that the smaller and more accurately portrayed decoys could then do their own attracting. Lincoln is also well known for what is often termed the "self-bailer" style of decoy: essentially a hollow-body design with the back end open to permit water to flow in and out freely.

If one can say that there is a typical Lincoln carving, then it is well represented in the Black Duck pictured here. As with most of his work, there is a stark simplicity about the piece that is at first deceptive. A closer examination of this and other examples soon reveals, however, that substantial thought and effort went into each design and its execution. Typically, the best decoy makers made the process appear easier than it was.

RED-BREASTED MERGANSER HEN
Joseph W. Lincoln
Accord, Massachusetts
c. 1920; Length, 18"

Whether an old decoy is viewed as art or artifact, there's no denying the strong sense of obligation many feel today to preserve and protect the best of this extraordinary American legacy. Happily, this conservation impulse is becoming common in our society as we begin more and more to recognize the need for preserving a continuity between past and present. It's a bit sobering, however, to realize that the objects we now choose for this special care will reveal more about our values and judgment to those who come after us than we might care to admit.

What follows are a few thoughts on the responsibilities of collecting and their practical application. Inasmuch as people often like to improve things, the danger exists that this noble instinct will lead some to do real harm. Decoys should never be altered to distort either the maker's intent or the signs of normal use, which are the visual record of its history. Of course, there will be times when other interests appear to conflict. For example, if accident or abuse results in such serious damage that a piece's resemblance to the original becomes tenuous, restoration would appear to be necessary. More typically, however, hard use over the years will have caused the paint to chip and wear away, as it has begun to do on Joe Lincoln's merganser decoy. In this case it is not a question of abuse, and the decision must be made as to whether or not a touchup of the painted surface is valid.

A decision about restoration must rest on a rigorous survey of the actual extent of damage. If one finds that the essence of the artist's work is seriously distorted, then restoration is usually justified. A head separated from a body and a bill completely broken off serve as uncomplicated illustrations. But if nothing more than honest wear exists, the decoy is best left alone. Otherwise, many problems will inevitably beset the overzealous fixer when he tries to transform a decoy into something it is not.

OLDSQUAW DRAKE
Lothrop Holmes
Kingston, Massachusetts
c. 1900; Length, 13½"

Decoys from New England provide an endless variety of forms, sizes, and attitudes to delight the discerning collector. Some of the most unusual decoys made anywhere hail from this rockbound coast, and Lothrop Holmes of Kingston, Massachusetts, contributed generously to this distinctive array.

While little is known about the man himself, his decoys have reached an eminence achieved by few other carvers. Especially noteworthy was the inclusion of two Holmes mergansers in an exhibition at The Metropolitan Museum of Art in New York City—a first for decoys. The Oldsquaw drake shown opposite is another Holmes masterpiece, a marvel of creative engineering. While this type of canvas construction probably did not originate with Holmes, it was used by him to the best possible effect. Joe Lincoln, the famed Accord, Massachusetts, maker produced numerous canvas-over-frame decoys, but

none is more beautiful than this Oldsquaw. It is, after all, an extraordinary idea: to construct a decoy body in somewhat the same way one would a modern building. How could a maker possibly justify this outpouring of effort except to have the lightest imaginable decoy? As one might expect, this method of construction never became dominant in any region, and in fact, most of Holmes's decoys had solid bodies.

Noteworthy too is the fact that Lothrop Holmes branded his duck decoys with his own name, a practice rarely encountered in any area. Although you won't find the same brand on his shorebirds, you shouldn't have any trouble identifying their maker, for the winning mix of bold forms, smooth surfaces, and stylishly decorative paintwork easily sets the shorebirds apart from those of any other maker.

LONG-BILLED CURLEW
Maker unidentified
Possibly Duxbury, Massachusetts, area
c. 1900; Length, 14″

It would be difficult to confuse curlews with other shorebirds, either as live birds or as decoys, for the length of the largest Atlantic coast curlew, the Long-billed, is nearly two feet from the tip of the bill to the end of the tail. All three types of curlew—the Long-billed (or "Sicklebill," as hunters liked to call it), Hudsonian, and Eskimo (the smallest of the three)— endured such relentless hunting during most of the last century that by 1900 the Eskimo had completely disappeared. Even today, the Long-billed Curlew is rarely sighted, although the Hudsonian's remarkable comeback means it is no longer endangered.

Because of the early disappearance of the Eskimo Curlew (it was the only edible one of the three), those decoys that have survived were probably used to hunt the other two types. If you should discover a small curlew decoy, its size alone will not justify the label Eskimo.

Curlew decoys taken as a group are not plentiful, and extremely well-carved and painted ones are exceptional rarities. Collectors searching for the best examples will look for those having a large and well-formed body, accurately patterned cinnamon-brown plumage, and a gracefully curved bill. The bill in particular should be original to the decoy, and ideally its most dramatic feature.

Most curlew decoys are by unidentified makers, as is the case with the striking Massachusetts decoy shown here. Strangely, curlew decoys by a number of major carvers, including George Boyd, Elmer Crowell, Joe Lincoln, and Ira Hudson, are yet to be found, although the reason for their absence is unclear.

LESSER YELLOWLEGS
Maker unidentified
Probably Massachusetts
c. 1910; Length, 12"

Powerful traditions were at work in all parts of the country, wherever wildfowl hunting and decoy making existed. A man growing up close to the water generally knew the local styles for decoys, boats, hunting techniques, and any other facts important to that area's prosperity. The decoy collector soon discovers that in each region there existed a clearly identifiable carving tradition, and simultaneously, a group of iconoclasts who largely ignored that tradition.

There is no need to wax poetic over the perky yellowlegs shown on the next page, for by most standards it is only an average decoy. Of chief interest here is the idiosyncrasy of its applied wings. This method of construction had been tried in several regions but never really caught on. Everywhere, individualists made what might be called false starts. In one place, a man made a shorebird and covered it with burlap, or flock, or leather. Elsewhere, he carved thighs and even legs. He applied horsehair or leather for merganser crests, pieces of tin for wing tips, and real feathers at the tail. He did what pleased him or what was necessary to make the wrong materials right. He simplified, complicated, exaggerated, flattened, attenuated—did anything that might work. More often than not his experiments failed or at least made no lasting contribution to the art of decoy making. His ideas have been rejected a thousand times, only that a few might survive and gain favor.

Today, the eccentric piece is generally passed over in favor of the tried-and-true work of established carvers. A modestly funded collector could assemble a unique and satisfying collection by selecting the best examples of these unusual decoys.

LESSER YELLOWLEGS
Maker unidentified
Massachusetts
c. 1910; Length, 12″

In late April, along the Massachusetts coast, the yellowlegs returns from its wintering places in the south to the shallow brackish waters and mud flats of New England. Several more weeks pass before other shorebirds appear, mostly plover. Numbers increase steadily until the end of May and then drop off dramatically as the birds fly farther north to breeding grounds in Canada. The adult yellowlegs will not be seen again until its return in September.

The two kinds of yellowlegs are the Greater, nearly fourteen inches long, and the Lesser, ten inches long. Distinguishing one type from the other can be difficult, for their markings are nearly identical. The Lesser is a more gregarious bird and is inclined to form larger flocks than its more cautious relative. The Greater is particularly adept at feeding in tidal ponds, often walking in up to its belly and occasionally even swimming. Both types eat snails, small fish, insects, worms, and crustaceans; and their long legs are especially useful in probing the bottoms of ponds.

Decoys for the Lesser and Greater Yellowlegs can be distinguished only on the basis of their size. If you see what appears to be an exceptionally large Greater Yellowlegs decoy, chances are that it's really a Willet. Except for this minor qualification, yellowlegs decoys will not normally be confused with those of any other species.

In the nineteenth century, decoys for the yellow-legs could be crudely carved and either painted badly or not at all. The live birds had not yet learned to fear the hunter. That situation, however, was short-lived as their numbers dwindled and their wariness increased in proportion, so by 1900 only the best decoys gave any hope of a successful hunt. Carvers varied poses, refined carving and painting techniques, and contributed to what eventually came to be recognized as a golden age of shorebird-decoy production. Preeners, runners, and feeders joined the decoy family in substantial numbers, all to the collector's delight.

LESSER YELLOWLEGS
Maker unidentified
Massachusetts
c. 1900; Length, 12½"

It has always seemed to me that civilization's advance generally depends less on the strength of individual genius than on that of collective achievement. Naturally, there are notable exceptions to this statement, with the decoy world included. Albert Laing of Stratford, Connecticut, is credited with having devised the famed Stratford model, so perfect from its inception that successors had little reason over the years to alter it. Generally, however, regional decoys developed more from an accumulation of individual responses to local needs than from one outstanding stroke of creativity.

The esteem in which a region's decoys are held appears largely determined by the strength and quality of that area's traditions. Superlative decoy making is typically a reflection of the ability and willingness of a carver's neighbors to support and encourage the finest work. Poorer and more isolated areas tended to be less nurturing, the decoy output was often more pedestrian, and the few premier makers were more detached from local practices.

Massachusetts, whose carvers may have produced more beautiful decoys than those of any other state, represents one of the most fertile locales for development of the decoy arts. The yellowlegs illustrated here shows several important Massachusetts shorebird characteristics: split-tail carving, smoothly finished surfaces, and a delicately sinuous form. Our anonymous maker had no reason to anguish over these matters of style, for they had already been included in the local carving vocabulary. His acceptance of their beauty and utility permitted him to craft a striking decoy. In fact, he probably felt compelled to.

BUFFLEHEAD DRAKE (left); BUFFLEHEAD HEN (right)
John Winsor
Duxbury, Massachusetts
c. 1890; Length of hen, 9½";
Length of drake, 11"

Decoy making is not an easy task. The skills of the designer, sculptor, carpenter, and painter must be expertly combined before a masterful decoy can take form. As in most arts, mediocre examples far outnumber truly superior ones, and even the best carvers had to learn from their mistakes. It thus seems probable that the first efforts of even the most talented makers would be found deficient in some important respect. In light of these assumptions the work of John Winsor appears all the more remarkable.

Virtually nothing is known about Winsor except that he was from Duxbury, Massachusetts, and that he made a splendid rig of Bufflehead decoys for his own use. They are of such quality that one immediately wonders how he came by his skills. It is difficult to believe that Winsor could prove this expert without a good deal of practice, yet these decoys are apparently the only ones he ever made. Even if one feels that there must have been other decoys by him, the number has to be very small, or else some of them would surely have shown up in collections by now.

So it appears obvious, therefore, that a few decoy craftsmen like John Winsor were able to make exceptional decoys right from the start and not experience the years of trial and error that surely dogged the average carver. And if there was the occasional piece that didn't quite live up to expectations, a quick trip to the woodstove was probably as far as it ever got.

RED-BREASTED MERGANSER HEN
Maker unidentified
Massachusetts
c. 1920; Length, 19"

Perhaps it was the sinuous shape of the body, or the crest at the back of the head (not seen on this example), or the especially vivid plumage of the drake that so excited decoy carvers when they made mergansers. Whatever the source of inspiration, merganser decoys unquestionably constitute one of the most expressive groups of carvings for any species. One can actually sense a depth of feeling about the best of them that is almost poetic, an uncommon quality in wildfowl art.

The live merganser is far more appealing to look at than to eat, for its steady diet of fish imparts a strong taste of the sea. Plant-eating ducks, especially the freshwater variety, invariably make better eating.

Nonetheless, when hunters lived by the ocean and mergansers were there to be taken, they inevitably were, and decoys were made to lure them.

Most merganser decoys that the collector encounters today are the Red-breasted type. Decoys for the Common and Hooded varieties were infrequently used because of the isolated nature of their lake and pond habitats. If you are lucky enough to acquire as fine a merganser as the hen decoy pictured, and you're not sure what kind you have, in all likelihood it is a Red-breasted. Common and Red-breasted mergansers (hens in particular) look very much alike, and few carvers ever felt the need to distinguish between them.

DOWITCHER
Attributed to William Henry Weston
Duxbury, Massachusetts
c. 1890; Length, 8"

Feeder, runner, turned head, sleeper, hisser, preener, swimmer, reacher—what delight decoy collectors take in describing ducks and shorebirds carved in unusual postures! And what pleasure they take in acquiring decoys like these, for they add immeasurable interest to any collection.

If one surveyed all the thousands of decoys made in the past hundred years, certainly the vast majority would be found in the conventional straight-ahead and upright pose; yet anyone who has observed groups of live ducks on the water or shorebirds congregating near beaches and tidal pools knows how unusual it is to find most of them staring directly forward. How strange then that most of the men who observed these delightful creatures would choose to make replicas that did not reflect a variety of attitudes. Of course, such renowned carvers as Elmer Crowell and Shang Wheeler often made duck decoys with naturally posed, lifelike heads, but they were the exceptions. Even Joe Lincoln, the famed Accord, Massachusetts, carver, rarely had his decoys looking anywhere but to the front. Actually, the majority of makers had quite enough trouble shaping a convincing head to fit well with a somewhat more easily formed body, without further complicating matters. Those who had the requisite skills and the willingness to exert themselves, and yet never altered a posture, are the great puzzle.

So it is the fortunate collector who has acquired a shorebird as graceful and pleasing as the Dowitcher by William Henry Weston. Feeders as beautiful as this one are indeed rare birds! Collectors have come to discover, to their dismay, that there are simply not enough treasures like this to go around.

LESSER YELLOWLEGS
Maker unidentified
Massachusetts
c. 1910; Length, 11½"

What decoy collector has not agonized over a trade or a purchase, while puzzling over the criteria that should guide his decision? The formula he seeks does not, of course, exist in any simple form. Yet there are very specific qualities that affect the worth of a decoy, and one of the most important of these is its condition.

The physical integrity of a decoy is crucial, so much so that when in some significant way it is compromised by damage, its desirability is seriously diminished. While sensitive restoration may help mitigate the problem, the need for extensive repairs generally persuades the wise collector to consider a different example. Certainly, the great rarity of a piece may obviate this point entirely, but such an exception generally proves the rule.

The condition of the painted surface and the quality of its patina are also important considera-tions, the former showing the maker's intent and the latter resulting from the decoy's life and use. The yellowlegs decoy illustrated here is original in all respects. That is indeed fortunate, for the quality of the carving and painting are worth preserving. The value of the piece is further enhanced by the deep, pleasing patina that shows so beautifully its age and the care it was given.

In some regions, decoys were repainted every year, making completely original examples either rare or nonexistent. As a matter of fact, the work of some important makers has never been found in original paint. Such extrinsic factors as these become important elements in any equation that attempts to evaluate the relative merits of collectible decoys. The sensible collector, then, will always temper his expec-tations with the reality born of knowledge and experience.

OLDSQUAW DRAKE (front); OLDSQUAW HEN (rear)
David Goodspeed
Duxbury, Massachusetts
c. 1890; Length of both, 12″

A thousand years ago, North American Indians hunted with decoys. This fact was established after scientists from the Museum of the American Indian in New York City discovered a group of eleven decoys that had survived for centuries in a Nevada cave. The decoys were constructed of bulrush, some covered with duck skins, others artfully bound in the shape of Canvasback ducks and decorated with feathers and native paints. This discovery became all the more remarkable for the fact that in Europe, where one might expect to discover our decoy-making antecedents, hunters invariably tethered live birds as decoys until at least the last century.

The basic form of the duck decoy and the use of skins and feathers are Indian concepts that have persisted into the modern era. As late as this century, Ojibwa Indians still attached real duck wings to pieces of corklike bark, while the Chippeway of Saskatchewan (Canada) employed the simple expedient of mounting the heads of real ducks on sticks that were pushed into the ground.

White hunters eventually appropriated many of the Indian methods, including the use of bird skins, wings, or feathers tacked on wooden bodies. Yet the ephemeral nature of these materials stood at odds with the white man's preference for permanent lures, and all-wood decoys finally won favor over the earlier types.

David Goodspeed's Oldsquaw decoys are powerful symbols of both the final ascendancy of the wooden decoy in American wildfowling as well as the unquestioned importance of the Native American legacy. It is interesting to note that Goodspeed drilled several holes at the back of each decoy so that he could insert tail feathers taken from a real Oldsquaw. It was an old idea that was still alive.

GREATER YELLOWLEGS
Russell Pratt Burr
Hingham, Massachusetts
c. 1910; Length, 12½"

Russ Burr and his uncle Elisha, both from the town of Hingham, Massachusetts, carved some of the most easily recognizable and pleasing shorebirds in all New England. An unusual "drop" tail and two other refinements—carved wing tips and overhanging wing primaries—were special marks of the Burr style. Unfortunately, the drop tail is also the most vulnerable part of their carvings, and many examples are found today with at least a portion of this tail section damaged. Only the New Englander's habit of taking good care of his decoys has permitted a few of these pieces to survive intact.

Miniature bird carvings were another significant part of Russ Burr's repertoire, covering the full range of waterfowl, game birds, and eastern songbirds. It is surprising to learn then that the man who carved so many shorebirds and decorative miniatures produced only one documented rig of duck decoys. George Ross Starr, the well-known Massachusetts historian of decoys, knew Russ Burr personally and was told by him that the only duck decoys he ever made were a few Black Ducks given to a hunting companion. Starr has also said that a friend of his was able to identify positively several of Burr's shorebird decoys because he had actually watched Burr make them.

Firsthand information like this illustrates the kind of personal knowledge of the old-time carvers that is so valuable to the decoy student and collector. Unfortunately, these connections to the past will soon disappear, leaving important history still unwritten.

BLACK-BELLIED PLOVER
Elisha Burr
Hingham, Massachusetts
c. 1910; Length, 11½"

When the art of making shorebird decoys had progressed beyond the most primitive stages, the carvers began to replicate more accurately both the natural form of the bird and the details of its plumage. At first, an upright pose was usually adopted for an entire group of decoys, with each bird invariably facing straight ahead. Occasionally, a maker would abandon the formula and add a few unusual postures to vary his rig. Elisha Burr went a step further, however, with a deceptively simple technique: he elongated the shorebird's body slightly and varied the angle of the head and bill to produce a variety of running and feeding attitudes.

To emphasize further the forward-reaching impression of the carvings, he chose an unusual placement for the tenon hole on the bottom of the decoy.

Most makers located the hole near the midpoint of the body, but Burr often placed it farther back, at the same time varying subtly the angle at which it entered the body. These clever manipulations, together with the "leaning into the wind" look of the decoys themselves, made possible a range of poses that derived from one relatively simple form.

Elisha and his nephew Russ Burr made shorebirds so much alike that it is now difficult to distinguish between them. It would seem that the two men were in complete agreement as to what constituted an effective shorebird decoy. Greater and Lesser Yellowlegs and plover were made by the Burrs, yet only a few carry an *E. Burr* brand. Today's collector is forced to compare his decoy with documented examples and draw his conclusions accordingly.

BLACK-BELLIED PLOVER
A. Elmer Crowell
East Harwich, Massachusetts
c. 1910; Length, 10″

When William Mackey, Jr., wrote *American Bird Decoys* in 1965, several Black-bellied Plover decoys by Elmer Crowell were illustrated on the dust jacket. Mackey chose wisely, for by general agreement these carvings are among the best shorebird decoys ever made. This was clearly Crowell decoy making at its peak, complete with lifelike postures, masterly brushwork, and beautiful detail. Indeed, these decoys became so fixed and famous in collectors' minds that soon they were known as "dust-jacket plovers."

Many Crowell shorebirds are found today in nearly perfect condition, which can be explained in two ways. The earliest gunning birds often so impressed their owners that they were reluctant to expose them to the bumps and bruises of hunting. A substantial number of these decoys came to rest on mantels and shelves without ever seeing a day's use. After shorebird gunning was outlawed in 1918, Crowell shifted to carving for the tourist trade, and these birds obviously were intended just for display. Crowell's decorative shorebirds were made either with the traditional hole in the bottom or with lifelike legs permanently affixed to a wooden base. Once in a while someone will remove the legs and drill a center hole in a later carving and thus try to pass it off as a true working Crowell. This is especially shameful, for the decorative pieces have their own undeniable merit and charm without having to serve as impostors.

Crowell made several grades of working shorebirds, the differences among them found mostly in the detailing of the carving and painting. The quality of workmanship on any of his decoys never varied, from the lowest grade Black Duck to the exquisite "dust-jacket" plover shown here. The obvious importance of the Crowell accomplishment can be put quite simply: in its combination of quality, quantity, and variety his work is unequaled by any other maker.

BLACK-BELLIED PLOVER (detail)
A. Elmer Crowell
East Harwich, Massachusetts
c. 1910; Length, 10″

Rarely was a decoy maker trained as an artist, so painting techniques were mostly of the self-taught variety. Carvers learned soon enough, however, that simple, abstract plumage patterns were very effective in attracting the live birds, and they adopted this shorthand, which most of them could easily hope to master.

Occasionally, however, a born artist arose from the ranks, and he would always be dissatisfied with the normal methods of creating decoys. Elmer Crowell was such a man, and while his carving conforms admirably to New England traditions (for this was his lesser strength), his approach to painting, with an emphasis on creating the most lifelike effect possible, made his work extraordinary. The naturalness of his color and surface has been equaled by no maker before or since.

Crowell's technique for painting shorebirds was deceptively simple. First came a base coat that was allowed to dry thoroughly; next, thick daubs of subtle, well-chosen colors were applied and left to become tacky. At this point Crowell used a completely dry brush to spread the colors so that each would meld with the others and yet retain the delicate striations made by the hairs of the brush. This technique simulated the look of real feathers, yet it was never successfully copied by any other maker. Perhaps that too can be called the highest form of flattery.

LESSER YELLOWLEGS
A. Elmer Crowell
East Harwich, Massachusetts
c. 1910; Length, 12″

The earliest shorebird decoys were make-do objects that only faintly resembled long-legged birds standing on the ground. A newly killed bird that was propped up or even a handful of grass tied on a stick might be used to lure unwary shorebirds. But these quick solutions obviously were only temporary, and the hunter depended on his luck of the moment in finding suitable materials. Eventually, primitive wooden decoys evolved, although at first no particular species was represented. These early wooden pieces had flat bodies and unpainted surfaces. Hunters soon began attaching feathers or actual wings to the wooden forms and finally started painting simple plumage patterns for the more commonly hunted birds.

Later, bodies and heads became more fully developed, although they were made separately and then joined. Roots with appropriate shapes were chosen and whittled a bit here and there, and they made fine, strong heads. Finally, the fully formed one-piece body became the dominant type; still, a design that was used at the beginning continued as a favorite. This was the flat shorebird decoy, or "flattie." Its chief advantage was the ease with which it could be made, and the fact that a large number of them could be conveniently transported and stored.

Elmer Crowell's flattie yellowlegs is a superior example of a simple form that never lost its appeal.

DOWITCHER
A. Elmer Crowell
East Harwich, Massachusetts
c. 1915; Length, 12″

Elmer Crowell made shorebird carvings even after gunning for the live birds was outlawed in 1918. This was not done to supply an illicit market, but to find a new audience after the old one had been legislated out of existence. The older working decoys and the new, purely decorative pieces soon became readily distinguishable.

Most experienced collectors today feel that Elmer Crowell's later shorebirds lost some of their appeal when compared to the working decoys. Bodies generally became thinner and more delicate, while plumage patterns had less of the earlier spontaneity and freshness as detail work became fussier.

Crowell's Dowitcher decoy is a transitional carving, displaying some of the virility of his earlier work with a measure of the new refinement found in the later examples. It possesses enough of the best qualities from each period, however, to deserve a place among the finer examples of Crowell shorebirds.

COMMON GOLDENEYE HEN
A. Elmer Crowell
East Harwich, Massachusetts
c. 1910; Length, 12½"

A trap awaits any new collector whose knowledge and experience are not yet a match for his enthusiasm. Often, the temptation is to build a collection quickly, and many reason that any decoy by a famous maker is sure to be a good choice. Oldtimers in the field sometimes call these neophytes "name" or "textbook" collectors because of their inclination to seek out what they believe to be the tried and true. Sadly, many pay dearly for mediocre examples of an illustrious maker's work.

The duck decoys made by Elmer Crowell during his long and productive career represent a sizable accomplishment, and many pieces remain to be collected. Yet it must be noted that with Crowell there was always a close connection between the effort he expended and the price he charged. Also, as time went by, the market changed considerably, with hunting-decoy business declining and decorative or ornamental pieces finding increasing favor. As a result, Crowell's ducks eventually came to be more pleasing to the tourist than to the hunter. So Elmer Crowell's duck decoys vary in their appeal, and a good deal of knowledge is necessary before wise choices are possible. Careful study should be made of Crowell's finest style, exemplified by the Goldeneye here. As in all areas of collecting, one should never miss the opportunity to train one's eye so thoroughly that making the necessary distinctions between *good*, *better*, and *best* gradually becomes instinctive.

RED-BREASTED MERGANSER DRAKE
A. Elmer Crowell
East Harwich, Massachusetts
c. 1910; Length, 19½"

The standards that are currently used to judge hand-made decoys are decidedly different from those relied upon in the past. Formerly, utilitarian concerns occupied the hunters: matters of a decoy's weight, durability, or any other aspect that related directly to the practicalities of hunting. Eventually, however, these old wooden birds came out of the water, and many ended up on the shelf. No longer just images of the live birds, they had also become sculptural symbols of the entire wildfowl-hunting era.

The attention of collectors soon began to focus on individual carvers. Specific regional and individual carver's characteristics became familiar, and so began the task of cataloging this vast army of wooden birds. The new research cultivated an awareness of the individuality of each maker, and as time passed, it became generally recognized that this decoy legacy was truly a bounty of creative artistic expression.

The extraordinary Elmer Crowell merganser pictured here would surely have passed the severest test of the hunter, although its present admirers are scarcely interested in that point. This decoy is now prized because it is a carving that is both uniquely conceived and beautifully realized.

GOLDEN PLOVER
Maker unidentified
Nantucket Island, Massachusetts
c. 1910; Length, 11½"

Sitting serenely twenty-five miles off the coast of Cape Cod, the island of Nantucket has always seemed a world apart. The whaling trade dominated life there during the last century, while shorebirds occupied the minds of the island's hunters. Even at that time, however, the Golden Plover was not plentiful, although they were sometimes seen making a meal of grasshoppers in local pastures. Today, fields on the island are still dotted with the pits dug by hunters a hundred years ago to conceal themselves.

By the late 1800s, heavy spring shooting along the Mississippi migratory route had almost made the Golden Plover extinct, so the use of Golden Plover decoys declined. Hunters then turned their guns on the Golden's slightly larger cousin, the Black-bellied Plover.

Distinguishing Golden Plover decoys from Black-bellieds usually depends on whether golden-yellow or greenish-yellow speckles or dots are on the back of the bird. If the markings are there, you have a Golden. Rarely, however, will one find the plover's characteristic bold white stripe over the eye, which is so prominent on the fine example pictured here. When the intrepid collector has identified his decoy as a Golden Plover yet remains uncertain as to whether or not it is a Nantucket bird, he will find this question of origin not so easily answered. You see, the island's snipe decoys simply have no common denominator: some are hollow, while others have solid bodies; some are one piece, some not; a number have separate heads, but more do not; many boast split tails, yet others do not; and so forth. Also, there was no well-known maker at work on the island: no Crowell or Lincoln that would simplify the task of determining origin.

Therefore, the solution to identifying one's latest acquisition may well require a visit to a senior collector familiar with Nantucket decoys. It may be encouraging to learn that the service is generally free and given with pleasure.

RED-BREASTED MERGANSER DRAKE (front)
RED-BREASTED MERGANSER HEN (rear)
Captain Osgood
Salem, Massachusetts
c. 1880; Length of both, 18½"

These decoys by Captain Osgood are in a class by themselves. Because they are handsome and dramatic pieces of sculpture, they generate remarkable interest among collectors, yet their origin remains clouded. What little is known has come to us in the form of a tradition stating that Osgood, a Salem, Massachusetts, sea captain, carved a group of Canada Goose decoys aboard ship during a layover on the California coast. Upon his return, he is said to have taken them to a friend's hunting lodge, where they remained for a hundred years.

Because so little is known about Osgood, it is probably inevitable that his decoys have been largely removed from their historical context and elevated to a special aesthetic status. Undeniably beautiful though they are, this particular emphasis may actually have contributed to our continuing lack of knowledge about this great carver's life and art.

The number of decoys now attributed to Osgood includes the five Canada Geese now at the Shelburne Museum and a relatively small number of Red-breasted Mergansers found in various collections. All are monumental in scale and obviously the work of a highly skilled hand. They are truly superior examples of American folk art.

BLACK-BELLIED PLOVER
George Boyd
Seabrook, New Hampshire
c. 1910; Length, 11″

In the first decade of this century, customers shopping for decoys at the Iver Johnson sporting goods store in Boston, Massachusetts, had an enviable choice. If duck decoys were on their list, Elmer Crowell's handiwork was available. Yellowlegs and plover decoys were supplied by a man later dubbed "the Elmer Crowell of the North Shore," George Boyd.

Boyd, a shoemaker in Seabrook, New Hampshire, turned his attention to decoy making quite early and produced a large number of yellowlegs and plover decoys of meticulous quality. His Canada Geese, Red-breasted Mergansers, Black Ducks, and Golden-eyes also exhibited a level of excellence in design and finish that was unmatched by all but a few makers. Even his canvas-covered Canada Goose and Black Duck decoys proved to be exemplary interpretations of this Massachusetts invention.

The painting of shorebirds especially was for Boyd an exercise in patience and precision. Hundreds of tiny brushstrokes formed a mosaic that deftly imitated the actual plumage. As no other species have come to light, his shorebirds apparently were limited to plovers and yellowlegs. And because many examples are found today in such excellent condition, it seems obvious they were often used for mantel decorations.

The Boyd signature for shorebirds, in addition to distinctive paintwork, is a squarish head with low-placed bill that makes them easy to distinguish from the work of other makers. Their undeniable charm and quality have also made them especially popular with collectors.

LESSER YELLOWLEGS
George Boyd
Seabrook, New Hampshire
c. 1910; Length, 11"

Even an experienced student of decoys finds it difficult to imagine a time (not much more than twenty years ago, certainly not before 1960) when the name George Boyd was unfamiliar. Mind you, this would have been true when the names of other important carvers were already well known. William J. Mackey, Jr., included pictures of Boyd's yellowlegs and plover in his book *American Bird Decoys* and observed that they were "shorebirds by a prolific, but unknown maker." How could it happen that a carver from New Hampshire whose decoys are so exceptional and so numerous would remain anonymous until as late as 1960? A brief account will help explain.

Joel Barber, the urbane architect from Wilton, Connecticut, was the first to discover and write about the unique qualities of American bird decoys. That was in the 1930s, and thirty more years passed before a new group of collectors, including Mackey and Adele Earnest, expanded Joel Barber's vision. Their books marked the start of a more comprehensive approach to the study of decoys. Still, there was an incompleteness about them that, when viewed in perspective, was a natural preliminary to today's more systematic work in the field. Twenty-five years ago, some makers were accorded more attention than their work merited, while others did not receive their due. Some, like Boyd, hadn't even been discovered. These imbalances have largely been righted in the last several years, but we continue to see parallels in other less-studied regions where decoy knowledge is spotty and perspective is absent. In retrospect, however, one marvels at the pioneer writers, these men and women of vision who willingly faced the demanding task of bringing order to a most complex subject.

RED-BREASTED MERGANSER DRAKE
Maker unidentified
Monhegan Island, Maine
c. 1890; Length, 16½"

Up along the New England coast, wildfowl gunning is very different from that on ponds and lakes, and so are the decoys. Here, the hunter is a sailor first, working to guide his dory through the rough, unsheltered waters out where the sea ducks congregate. A delicate decoy would quickly be lost to sight in the churn of the whitecaps. Seaworthiness, then, must be the primary quality of a decoy, and most of those found are best described as workmanlike.

Monhegan Island is not far from the mainland, yet it is a world apart. Decoys from the island are, as the early collector and author Joel Barber observed, "made seemingly for all time, heirlooms passed down from father to son." Monhegan's year-round population is about eighty, so the large number of rugged, sculptural decoys attributed to its carvers defies simple logic. In fairness, however, we should honor the work from the region that measures up to the island's standards and consider it part of the Monhegan school.

The Red-breasted Merganser shown opposite is a magnificent example of the island's best work. While it boasts all the important Monhegan characteristics—head mortised into the body, wide beam, flat bottom—the head especially draws our attention by its surpassing beauty. Tradition says that local makers bent and tied saplings to induce a pattern of growth that would eliminate the tricky crossgrain when the head and neck were carved from a single block of wood. This intuitive concern for structure and form, this bold architecture becoming the tradition for Monhegan carvers, often produced decoys of exceptional quality.

COMMON EIDER DRAKE
Maker unidentified
Maine or Nova Scotia
c. 1920; Length, 17"

The more one becomes involved with decoys, or any field of collecting, for that matter, the more information one wants and needs to acquire. In the past several years a large number of books and articles has appeared, some, of course, more helpful than others. A predictable result of this knowledge explosion in the decoy field is the sometimes unflattering light it casts on what was formerly held as gospel. The information about the monumental eider pictured here is a good example of my point.

A catalogue entry at the Museum of American Folk Art in New York City states that this decoy is the work of a Captain Obed of Nova Scotia. No apparent difficulty is caused by that attribution, especially as a Jesse Clayton Obed is known to have carved a number of eider decoys while working at a lighthouse on the South Shore of Nova Scotia. Also, this decoy and those illustrated elsewhere as being by Obed are strikingly similar. Everything fits beautifully until a closer examination reveals a series of subtle differences.

The first notable discrepancy is obvious only after it is mentioned: other eider decoys by Captain Obed have carved eyes, but this decoy has no eyes. Also, on the Obed decoys pegs are used to connect the inletted head and neck segments to the body, but none are found on this example. Finally, one can see a difference in the way the tails are formed: the Obed eiders have a squarer, more abruptly rising rear section. Add to all this the fact that some Maine and Nova Scotia decoys bear a striking resemblance to one another, and one realizes there are suddenly more questions about provenance than answers.

112

BROADBILL DRAKE
David K. Nichol
Smith Falls, Ontario
c. 1900; Length, 13″

Canadian decoys have never achieved the popularity in this country that their quality and originality deserve. No conspiracy is at work here, probably not even a chauvinism that might narrow the vision of collectors in the United States. It was, quite simply, not until recently that Canadian decoys had been carefully studied and written about in some depth; early writers in the field seemed to be completely unaware of significant accomplishments north of the border. One wonders how such an important hunting region along the Atlantic and Mississippi flyways could be ignored for so long. Perhaps the explanation is an obvious one: people know best what is close at hand. Early collectors were concentrated in the northeastern and central sections of the United States, leaving Canada, Louisiana, and areas farther west and all the way to the Pacific coast largely unexplored.

The last great frontier for decoy collectors is surely the Canadian provinces. Here, the range of invent-iveness and undeniable quality compares favorably with fine decoy work in the United States. In Ontario alone, nearly a dozen distinct styles have been identified, and a beginning has been made in the proper cataloguing of the region's carvers and their accomplishments.

The eastern end of Ontario near Smith Falls and the more western portion near Toronto provide an interesting contrast in styles and even cultures. English Protestants have dominated the culture in the Toronto area, while Smith Falls and environs are strongly influenced by the nearby province of Quebec. The areas could not be more different in their methods for making decoys. Toronto area carvers made a strikingly simple, smooth, and hollow decoy of the utmost restraint. Smith Falls carvers echoed Quebec makers with their elaborate portrayal of feathering. David Nichol's broadbill, in the Smith Falls style, exemplifies the best of the Canadian decoy-making tradition.

SELECTED REFERENCES

Barber, Joel. *Wild Fowl Decoys*. 1934. Reprint. New York: Dover Publications, 1954. Entertaining telling of the history and development of the decoy-making arts by this country's first collector.

Earnest, Adele. *The Art of the Decoy: American Bird Carvings*. 1965. Reprint. Exton, Pa.: Schiffer Publishing, Ltd., 1982. Consistently perceptive account of decoy-making traditions from a notable authority on American folk sculpture.

Haid, Alan G. *Decoys of the Mississippi Flyway*. Exton, Pa.: Schiffer Publishing, Ltd., 1981. A well-researched book that gives the decoys of this long-neglected flyway their due.

Mackey, William J., Jr. *American Bird Decoys*. New York: E.P. Dutton & Co., Inc., 1965. Still the best combination of a regional survey and the story of the decoy by this field's greatest authority.

Starr, George Ross, Jr. *Decoys of the Atlantic Flyway*. New York: Winchester Press, 1974. "Doc" Starr's travels up and down the Atlantic coast in search of decoys are recounted with style and wit.